Bill Holley

•

More than
a Doctor

QUA IBOE FELLOWSHIP
7 Donegall Square West
Belfast BT1 6JE

© 1991
First Published 1991
ISBN 0 9507657 6 7

Printed in Great Britain by Wright's (Sandbach) Ltd., Sandbach, Cheshire

Contents

Introduction

ON 1st January 1990, Ochadamu Medical Centre in Benue State, Nigeria, was given a new name – HOLLEY MEMORIAL HOSPITAL. Who was the man who, twenty-five years after his departure from Nigeria, was being honoured in this way? What made him so beloved by leprosy patients, alcoholics and prisoners, at home and overseas? This little book, written at the request of the Qua Iboe Church, is an attempt to answer these questions and put on permanent record the story of Dr. Bill Holley – remembered by all who knew him as MORE THAN A DOCTOR.

Material has been drawn from Qua Iboe magazines, tapes and letters; from the memories of many friends and colleagues, and especially from Mrs. Marion Holley and other members of the family circle without whose help and support the project would have been impossible. I am also indebted to Mr. Alf McCreary for permission to quote from his book *Tried by Fire* (published by Marshall-Pickering); to Mr. Arthur Williams and Mr. James McIlroy for information about the Stauros Foundation and Prison Fellowship, and to personal friends who assisted with typing, photo-copying and checking of the script.

It would be Bill Holley's desire that all the praise for any good accomplished through his life should be passed on, untouched, to his Lord and Saviour, Jesus Christ.

Jean S. Corbett

CHAPTER ONE

The Reality of Jesus

THE YEAR was 1941 and the second World War had been raging for eighteen months. On the roof of a Belfast hospital, two young medical students were engaged in fire-watching. It had seemed a good idea to volunteer, for with the job came comfortable living quarters and some extra pay. They thought it highly unlikely that German bombers would ever reach Northern Ireland, but that night as they stood exposed to the full fury of the blitz they realised how mistaken they had been. Fear gripped their hearts as they scanned the familiar city that lay before them. Through recent months it had been shrouded in darkness because of the compulsory black-out. Now it was lit by falling flares and raging fires, the drone of enemy aircraft mingling with the wailing of sirens, the crack of anti-aircraft guns, and the sickening thud of exploding bombs. One of the fire-watchers later admitted that only the thought of having to pass the brave nurses at work in their busy wards kept him from deserting his post of duty and dashing for cover. His name was Bill Holley.

William Martin Holley had been born on the 2nd June 1917, in the pleasant town of Coleraine in Co. Londonderry, where his father, William John Holley, was a well-known and respected building contractor. He and his kindly wife, Elizabeth, with their four sons and one daughter, lived in a bungalow whose garden ran down to the river Bann. Later they moved to another home in the nearby sea-side resort of Portstewart, looking over a fine stretch of golden sand and rolling sea-breakers to the hills of Donegal.

William Holley, junior, received his early education at a local primary school before gaining entrance to Coleraine Academical Institution. A boyhood friend recalls how Willie, as he was then known, rode to school on his low-slung bicycle with racing-type handlebars and how, having earned a place on the 1st XV rugby team, he broke the news so sympathetically to another boy who had not been chosen. Even then he was showing the consideration that was to make him such a good doctor and well-loved man. Also remembered was his skill as an oarsman, and the broad grin he gave as his boat with its eight-man crew passed the cheering crowd on the river bank. Most of all, his friends still remember those bright eyes that twinkled with the Holley humour and kindliness.

Although he was a regular attender at New Row Presbyterian Church and the Sunday School where his father was a teacher, young Bill Holley did not yet know the Lord. Both his parents were followers of Christ and sought to introduce all their children to Him from earliest years, but Bill had formed the opinion that Christianity was a dull business – not for young fellows like him.

After a six months' trial period in his father's building firm, he left home to study medicine at Queen's University. With typical enthusiasm he threw himself into various student activities, playing games, gaining a 'blue' at football, and representing the University at different inter-varsity functions. But, in spite of all, he failed to find satisfaction. Thinking that the secret might lie in pleasures that his parents would have considered worldly, he threw off old restraints and determined to have as good a time as possible on his limited spending money of five shillings per week. He was popular with fellow students and, undoubtedly, there were spells of happiness, but these were very short lived. God was far from his thoughts, and he was doing barely enough work to scrape through his examinations.

It was in 1940 that he had the first of what he later described as 'three visitations of God'. In April of that year he was called home to see his mother who suddenly had been taken seriously ill. When she died, a few days later, Bill lost his closest friend and confidante. He realised then the awful separation that death brings and his own unreadiness for it. Trying to make himself right with God he decided to give up drinking and gambling, smoking and dancing. His good resolutions didn't last long. 'I'm too young for that sort of thing,' he reasoned. 'Time enough later on.'

Now, a year later, as the German flares fell around him for the third night in succession, God spoke to him again. That morning he had been called to examine the bodies of three young policemen, buried alive in the ruins of their station around the corner from the hospital. Sickened and horrified, he was brought face to face once more with the brevity of life and his own unpreparedness to meet his Maker. Fear of death was bad but fear of judgement was even worse. Dry-mouthed with terror the two students decided that they had better make their peace with God. There on the roof-top they knelt down and repeated the well-known words of John 3:16: *'For God so loved the world that He gave His only begotten Son, that whosoever believeth on Him should not perish but have everlasting life.'*

'Oh God,' they prayed, 'if you spare our lives, we'll give up all our bad habits and start going to church and reading the Bible and saying our prayers.' Surely that was a fair bargain, they reckoned.

For the next five days Bill struggled to give up smoking, biting his nails to ease the craving and suffering all the misery of withdrawal. Then came welcome news that, with the longer day-light hours of British summertime, the German bombers would be unlikely to return. That was all Bill needed. With relief he reached for his packet of cigarettes and forgot all about his vow. Christianity was for the select few, not for fellows like him.

When he had been qualified for a year, the war was still in progress, so Bill decided to join the armed forces. His brother was in the Royal Air Force but Bill chose the Royal Navy, first because he liked the uniform, and secondly because drink and tobacco were duty free! Then God intervened again. Shortly before he was due to leave, a Christian friend came to say good-bye. Before Bill could escape, he went on to speak about the Saviour.

'You know, Bill,' he said, 'the Lord Jesus is more real to me than you are.'

The young doctor was amazed. He had been used to thinking about Christianity as a set of 'do's and don'ts', not as a vital relationship with a living person. He was suddenly overwhelmed with a deep sense of need and of the reality of the living Christ.

'Look here, Sam,' he said, 'I've tried this thing before and it hasn't worked. How can you really get to know the Lord?'

'Well,' said Sam, 'you trust Him as your personal Saviour. He died for your sin and if you receive Him, He will come into your life and make you a new person.'

'But I'm smoking sixty cigarettes a day,' said Bill. 'Can He break that habit?'

'Yes,' said Sam, with confidence. 'Here's His promise from John 1:12: *"As many as received Him to them gave He power to become the sons of God, even to them that believe on His name."'*

That night, 10th August, 1942, under sudden but deep conviction of sin, Bill Holley knelt and committed himself unreservedly to Christ. As he rose from his knees his friend asked:

'Well, are you a Christian?'

'Yes!' said Bill, with a quiet assurance that surprised himself.

'How do you know?' Sam pressed him.

'Because God has said it and I believe His Word.'

Miracles of miracles, Bill Holley had become a new creation – a child of God!

A few minutes later the door bell rang and there stood another young doctor, who was going into the Royal Air Force. They were in process of arranging a farewell drinking party for their pals in a local hotel. He took one look at Bill and asked:

'What has happened to you?'

Bill mumbled something about having become a Christian.

'Oh well,' said his friend, 'if that's the way of it, I won't want to see you again; forget about the party.'

Old things were already passing away; all things had become new. But how could a young convert's faith survive in the Navy? Bill prayed fervently that God would deliver him from that obligation but, to his dismay, three weeks later, the call came to report to Portsmouth for six weeks' training in *H.M.S. Victory* before joining *H.M.S. Test,* an anti-submarine frigate, as surgeon-lieutenant.

Many years later, Bill recalled those days, when speaking to a group of young people. 'The name of the ship was appropriate,' he said, 'for during the next four years I was tested both physically and spiritually. Physically, it was tough, for I never was a good sailor. In heavy seas I went through two stages, first being afraid that the ship was going down and then being so sick that I wished it would! But, spiritually, it was a great time of proving God. Oh, the reality of Jesus as a living Saviour, constant companion, unchanging friend! True there was the stumbling and falling, but then getting up again, seeking forgiveness, and asking God's help to avoid making the same mistakes in the future!'

Two and a half years of Bill's war service were spent at Simonstown Naval base, near Capetown. While there, he received much teaching and encouragement from godly missionaries, which was to have a profound influence on the whole of his Christian life.

'Indeed,' he recalled, 'I look back on those war-time years in the Royal Navy as my Bible School, when God helped me to understand His Word and gave me the grace to serve Him.'

CHAPTER TWO

We're Going to Qua Iboe!

IT WAS Easter Monday, 1946. In a few weeks Dr. Bill Holley would be demobilised from the Royal Navy.

Today he was in Bangor, Co. Down, to take part in the annual Convention of the Faith Mission. As he came into the church with other speakers, all eyes were on the exceptionally handsome young man in naval officer's uniform. When eventually he rose to speak, however, appearances were forgotten. Here was a man to whom Jesus Christ was a living reality and whose burning desire was to serve this wonderful Lord and Master.

In the crowded congregation that day there was a young nurse on vacation from Ridgelands Bible College in England. Marion Jenks had been brought up in Belfast by dedicated Christian parents and from childhood had loved the Saviour. At the age of thirteen, with growing understanding, she had committed her life fully to Him and experienced a definite conversion. From then on, a deepening awareness of God's call to overseas service led her to enrol as a student in Belfast's Royal Victoria Hospital. After five years in nursing she had gone to Ridgelands, all the time continuing to grow in the knowledge of God's Word and devotion to the Saviour.

The Jenks' home was always open to missionary visitors. Many of them spoke to Marion about an urgent need for nurses in their area. At Bible College, too, she heard of worldwide opportunities, but as yet no clear guidance had been given concerning her own future service. All she knew was that she was available to God for whatever and wherever He chose, even if that should mean abandoning any thought of marriage.

But now here before her in the pulpit stood Bill Holley. For years she had known the name of the popular medical student but they had never met. One day, in 1942, she heard two young doctors discussing the sensational news that Holley had 'seen the light'. Consumed by curiosity about this dramatic change, they speculated about how long it would last in the Navy. Soon afterwards Marion read Bill's testimony in a small Forces magazine and bought some copies for the doctors whose conversation she had overheard.

Four years later, a fellow-student at Ridgelands told her about the Ulster-born surgeon-lieutenant and his Christian influence on board ship and at the naval base where they had met in South Africa. Small wonder then, that Marion was looking forward to seeing and hearing him that Easter Monday at Bangor.

As Bill traced the story of his conversion and spoke earnestly and eagerly of his desire to serve the Lord and suffering humanity, his words found a deep echo in her heart. After the meeting they were introduced by a mutual friend, and each recognised in the other the life partner of God's choice.

Demobilisation came on 1st May. Two months later Dr. Holley began a six months' appointment in Ards hospital, where he had previously worked in 1942-43. Friendship with Marion grew steadily and in December they became engaged to be married.

Soon afterwards Bill went to England for a four

months' course in the Liverpool School of Tropical Medicine. Wartime contacts with Africa had given him a love for the people of that great continent and he longed to use his medical knowledge to show the compassion of Christ – possibly to sufferers from leprosy in a pioneer situation. For this purpose some training in tropical medicine would be essential.

Together or apart, he and Marion were continuing to wait on God for His guidance. Eventually they decided to approach a well-known missionary society, but were told that it had no such work in prospect. A second enquiry also proved fruitless. What was God saying to them? How much longer must they wait? They were not looking for a dramatic revelation, but they firmly believed that through God's Word, through prayer, through circumstances, and through the quiet witness of the Holy Spirit in their hearts they would 'assuredly gather' His plan for their lives. Their part was to be wholly available to Him.

The annual Portstewart Convention has been the scene of many a spiritual battle and life-changing experience. On the last Thursday in June 1947, Bill Holley was among the great crowd in the big tent, listening to a notable and much-loved speaker, Canon Herbert W. Cragg. *'Speak to the children of Israel that they go forward,'* came the Word of God, and, deep within, came the prompting of the Holy Spirit – 'to Qua Iboe'. Bill had been sitting beside his future father-in-law. As they came out of the tent he surprised him by announcing, 'We're going to Qua Iboe!'

The Qua Iboe Mission had been familiar to both Bill and Marion since childhood. Indeed, Marion had been friendly with the daughter of the former General Secretary and was often with her in the Mission Office. Step by step they were being directed towards this Ulsterbased Mission. That night Bill sat down to write a letter, sharing his thoughts with his fiancée and wondering how she would react. Imagine his delight, two days later, to receive a letter telling how she had been reading in the Qua Iboe quarterly magazine of the need for leprosy work in Igala. She felt sure that this was God's place for them! In the providence of God their letters had crossed in the mail, bringing double confirmation that the call was truly from Him.

Soon they were filling in application papers and being interviewed by Home Council. This doctor and nurse came as an answer to many earnest prayers and were warmly welcomed into the Qua Iboe family. On 31st October they were united in marriage and in January 1948, Dr. and Mrs. Holley set sail for Nigeria.

At that time the hospital at Etinan needed a doctor so the new missionaries were located there for their first two years before moving to Igala. Soon after arriving, Marion wrote about their welcome at Aba.

'It would be impossible to give an adequate description of our sensations, but we felt *at home,* and rejoiced in the deepening consciousness that Nigeria is the place of *His* choice. The evangelist and several teachers live on the Mission compound, and Mrs. Graham introduced me to them and their wives. It filled my heart with joy to hear the evangelist say, "We have prayed for you so long, and now you have come to help us." We spent our first night at Aba but the heat and strangeness of everything made sleep difficult. Next morning we set out for Etinan and once we saw the hospital we realised without a doubt that, meantime, our place is here. The need is overwhelming – for workers, equipment, and new buildings. We ourselves wish we had half a dozen lives to give.'

Etinan hospital brought many experiences for which Dr. Holley felt ill-equipped. His training had been in medicine rather than surgery, but there was no-one else to do the work so he was soon immersed in operations, administration, post mortems and court cases. Years later he recalled it as a time of being 'cast wholly on the Lord, with the staff helping and supporting me.'

His programme included weekly visits to Ekpene Obom where Sister Edith Vear was caring for 200 leprosy patients, and also to several outstation clinics. One expedition was described in the Mission magazine:

'Having packed our medicines and stowed them with our bicycles into the Dodge kit-car, Sister Cairns and I, with two boy nurses, set out from Etinan at 7 am for Afaha Eket. Arrangements had been made for the people to gather in the church where we were met by the pastor. A congregation of more than six hundred people, including patients and their friends, awaited us. This was a wonderful opportunity to preach the Gospel, and I spoke from Mark 2 on the palsied man who had been brought to Jesus. The message seemed so applicable, as these folk also had come seeking physical healing, not realising their greater need of sins forgiven. After the service each patient was given a treatment card containing their name and reference number, as well as texts of Scripture, which we pray will continue to speak to them after we have left.'

In gathering darkness the medical team left for Ibeno, travelling the first four miles by kit-car and then by canoe and bicycle. After a welcome bath, meal, and night's rest, they were up at 5.30 am to see another three hundred patients before returning to Etinan.

'We reached home at 7.30 pm,' wrote Dr. Holley, 'tired, but with a deep satisfaction that comes from being labourers together with the Master in this great harvest field.'

One of the most harrowing experiences of the Holley's term at Etinan was the serious illness of Margaret Currie, the eleven-year-old daughter of Mr. and Mrs. Donald Currie, then living at Ikot Idong. At first her symptoms seemed to indicate a bad dose of malaria. Soon it became all too clear that she was suffering from the dreaded blackwater fever. Horrified at what he saw and realising his own inexperience, Dr. Holley sent an urgent appeal for help to the Church of Scotland Leprosy Settlement, over thirty miles away at Itu. Dr. McDonald responded immediately but there was little anyone could do apart from praying. Bill Holley's diary recorded his deepest fears and also his faith in the power of God:

"Outlook very grave – but GOD.'

'There is nothing too hard for the Lord – our eyes are towards Thee.'

A meeting of the Field executive had been arranged for that Saturday but, instead, the missionaries gave themselves to prayer. Next day the regular church services were abandoned so that hundreds of believers could spend the time in intercession. The little girl, struggling for life, was surrounded by a great wave of faith and love. By 12 noon the bleeding had ceased and she had begun a slow but sure return to health. Her mother recalls:

'Bill stayed with us for a week and it was such a comfort and joy to have him.'

She herself, as a nurse, had first recognised the illness and, turning in anguish to her *Daily Light,* had read: *'This sickness is not unto death but to the glory of God.'*

So indeed it proved to be. Marion Holley remembers: 'What a boost this was to the Nigerian Christians and missionaries alike! There was great rejoicing at the gracious answer from the Lord in sparing this young life. A renewed confidence in prayer and in a wonder-working God was given to us all.'

Shared anxieties can be used of God to unite His people, and shared joys can also strengthen the bonds of Christian fellowship. Both were being experienced at Etinan. The Holleys had been living in Matron Mary Russell's bungalow until their own house could be built and it was there, on 16th August 1948, that their first child was born. In a further token of the heavenly Father's loving provision, a new doctor, Esther Davis, had arrived a few weeks previously – just in time to assist at baby Rosemary's birth and to share in the general rejoicing.

Dr. Davis vividly remembers Bill's remarkable energy, and his determination never to get so absorbed in medical work that spiritual priorities would be neglected. In the cool of the dawn, he was to be found on the verandah with an open Bible, drawing strength for the demands of another busy day. Times of united prayer were carefully guarded too, and one petition often on his lips was that all their reactions, to each other and to every changing situation, might be 'in the Lord'. It wasn't enough to have become a man in Christ – there had to be a daily abiding in Him.

The reputation of the hospital was spreading and an increasing number of patients were coming for treatment. Aware of the pressing need for better accommodation, Home Council decided to sponsor a building programme in memory of the Mission's Founder and its first General Secretary, who had died within months of each other in 1942. In 1949 the new General Secretary, Mr. Isaac McEwan, on a visit to Nigeria, came to Etinan to lay the foundation stone of the S.A. Bill and R.L. McKeown Memorial Hospital – a memorable occasion for all who were present that day.

A new nurse, Dorothy Wetton, had arrived with Esther Davis, and now there was futher cause for rejoicing with the news that Dr. Oswald Mitchell felt God was calling him to serve at Etinan. Here was the answer to many prayers for a surgeon – and his fiancée was a nurse! With deep thankfulness Bill and Marion realised that now they would be free to move north to the place that still beckoned them – IGALA.

CHAPTER THREE

Ambassadors for Christ

IGALA WAS situated two hundred and fifty miles north of Etinan, bounded on the west by the Niger and on the north by the Benue river. Qua Iboe missionaries had first arrived there in 1931 and had found an encouraging response to the gospel message. Senior among them were Mr. and Mrs. Herbert Dickson, who were now living in the principal town of Idah and engaging in a widespread ministry of teaching, preaching and caring for the sick.

In 1947 Hilda Dickson had written about the plight of leprosy sufferers living in shacks near their house:

'There was not a Christian among them. We tried to pay regular visits and they brightened up considerably. One little girl always came running to meet us just because I had given her a Christmas card. Twenty have now been sent to Itu (three hundred miles away), but how great is the need of leprosy sufferers through all this area!'

A few months later Dr. and Mrs. Kearney were posted to Ankpa and, with the Dicksons, began to lay plans for leprosy clinics. Patients came from all over the country and it soon became obvious that a permanent settlement must be established. The task of finding a suitable site was entrusted to Hon. Peter Achimugu, a highly-respected elder in the church at Idah. This pioneer work would require its own doctor, someone with vision, energy and compassion – just the job for Bill Holley!

In preparation, the Holleys spent a month at the Church of Scotland Leprosy Settlement at Itu. Under the expert guidance of Dr. McDonald, Dr. Holley was able to observe the examination of patients prior to their discharge, and to learn much about treatment and rehabilitation.

It was now time for furlough so, towards the end of 1949, Marion sailed home, eager to introduce the year-old Rosemary to her waiting grandparents. Before joining them, Bill travelled north to survey the situation to which they hoped to return a few months later. From the beginning he loved Igala with its wide-open spaces and friendly people. The more he saw of its medical need the more convinced he became that this was indeed the place for which God had been preparing him.

In the autumn of 1950 the Holley family took up residence at Idah, in the house normally occupied by the Dicksons who were then on furlough. With them came Udofit, a Efik-speaking houseboy who, through their care at Etinan, had been cured of spinal tuberculosis. It was a big thing to ask him to live so far from home and Bill Holley never forgot the unhesitating reply, so typical of his own attitude – 'I am ready.'

A fine site had been secured for a leprosy settlement forty miles from Idah. The doctor's house was built of mud blocks and whitewashed, with a thatched roof. It was given the grand name of 'Gingham Grange' because every window had gaily-coloured curtains made from a generous gift of that material! The enthusiasm of those early days is evident in the following report, written by Dr. Holley in 1951:

'We are settled in our new house at Ochadamu, and

our hearts are full of praise to God for all His help. The Ata, or King-Priest of Igala, has given us two square miles of bush for colony development, and part of this is being cleared. Until now the patients have been living in grass huts, which are suitable only for the dry season. Last week, however, we transferred the men to five rows of mud houses, and preparations are being made to provide similar accommodation for the women.

'Opportunities for spiritual work are unique, for the majority of patients stay from eighteen months to two years. More than half the number already admitted are pagan, and, apart from a few Christians, the remainder are Muslims. Attendance at the meetings is entirely voluntary, and it is encouraging to see a full turn-out at both services on Sundays. Morning and evening prayers are held daily, and once a week there is a Bible class, a women's sewing class, a reading lesson, and also a prayer meeting. We believe that this concentrated sowing of the Word will yield a rich harvest.

'The days are busy, and a good deal of organisation is required in seeing to the occupational side of treatment. Most Igalas engage in farming, and for this reason it is the popular employment in our colony. An adjacent fast-flowing river provides a fishing ground, and there is, of course, road-making, building and basket-making to be done. Apart from those who have badly-affected feet or hands, there is no reason that any should be idle.'

Those were exciting days. As word spread about the loving care and effective treatment available at Ochadamu, requests for general medical clinics began to come in from as far as 180 miles away. In one month the doctor visited nine different centres and treated over

2,500 people. Many of them heard the gospel for the first time; some began to attend church; others asked for a teacher to be sent to their village.

In April 1951 a second daughter was born to the Holleys at Enugu Government Hospital. Elder Matthew, Igala's first elder, was there when the baby was brought home to Ochadamu. Taking her gently in his arms he dedicated little Alison to the Lord – a precious memory recalled by her father thirty years later.

With two small girls to care for, Marion Holley was fully occupied, but she also had a deep concern for the plight of Igala mothers who came seeking help. Many of them had lost child after child; some were being cast off by their husbands because of their failure to raise a family. Here was a ministry that a mother with nurse-training could undertake, literally on her own doorstep. So, on the back verandah of the doctor's house, the baby clinic was born. Mothers with babies came in their hundreds, often walking long distances to attend.

It soon became clear that there were two main causes of the high rate of infant mortality. One was tetanus through infection of the cord which was plastered with mud or cow dung. Another was malnutrition. The first breast milk was withheld because it was believed to be impure and when the starving baby failed to thrive it was forcibly fed with strong purgative medicine. In vain the Holleys tried to reason against these practices, but custom dies hard in any society. Then they had a brainwave:

'What if we made up a mixture to be given instead of the Igala medicine until the mothers feel it safe to breast-feed?'

It was worth a trial. Bottles were filled with water and a few spoonfuls of glucose. Every mother wanted it; every baby loved it; fathers travelled many miles to obtain the 'sweet medicine' for their offspring. And soon the results were visible in growing numbers of healthy children.

There was no limit to the demand for general medicine, but Bill Holley's foremost call was to 'heal the leprosy sufferer', and this must always be his priority. Injections were very popular but the new treatment was administered in tablet form. The doctor made a fair offer:

'I'll give you what you ask for if you'll take what you need!'

The bargain was acceptable and, oh, what an upsurge of hope as patients saw their patches of leprosy begin to disappear!

'But what about the sacrifice?' they would ask, remembering the demands of the native doctor.

With great joy, Bill Holley would assure them:

'The sacrifice has already been made. You don't need to bring a white turtle or any other offering. The Son of God loved you so much that He gave Himself as a sacrifice for sin, once for all. If you repent and believe in Him you can have something even better than healing from leprosy – forgiveness of sin and eternal life.'

At first there was no church at Ochadamu. In the evening the doctor and his helpers would go down to the patients' houses. A Tilley lamp would be put on a tall stand, low stools would be brought out, and pain and heartache would be forgotten as, in his own special way, Bill Holley told a story from the Bible and spoke about the Saviour's love. Jesus was so real to him that he was able to make His presence vividly real to others.

As numbers increased so did the need for a church where all could meet together. A dispensary was also needed for general patients. But even the simplest of buildings would cost £600. Where could the money be found? As usual, Dr. Holley rallied the Christians to pray. Before long an anonymous gift of £500 was received. Then, far away in Scotland, Mr. Dickson was handed an envelope containing a cheque. It was from the trustees of Shore Street Hall in Port Glasgow, founded by his father many years before, with the request that it should be used for some specific project in Nigeria. The cheque was for exactly £100. With much thanksgiving and many willing helpers, a beautiful mud church was erected, its high-pitched thatched roof blending perfectly with the trees that gave welcome shade in the developing compound.

One of the first services in the new church was described by Dr. Holley:

'Saturday, 19th April, 1952, will always be remembered as a very special day here at Ochadamu, when we had the great joy of handing out symptom-free certificates to seven of our patients – the first to return to their homes from this Settlement. What a thrill it was – this day for which we have been preparing during the past two years. How wonderful to see five men and two women free from the dreadful disease of leprosy, but far, far more wonderful to know that each one has been to Calvary for cleansing from sin!

'We all, working together, sought to have everything in order for the visitors. The grass was cut and all the roofs repaired. The new church was completed and preparations were made for the service to be held there. Our fifteen school children were supplied with new cloth for the occasion, while other patients were busy washing and mending their clothes in order to look their best.

'At last the great day dawned. During the morning there was a final inspection, when last-minute instructions were given concerning the afternoon's activities. Our missionaries began to arrive, and after lunch we welcomed the Ata and his nine councillors. These, with their flowing robes and head-dresses, added much colour to the scene. Together we visited the patients' quarters, and then returned to meet the District Officer, with other Government officials and traders from Idah.

'Proceeding to the church, which was already filled to capacity, we found outside many of the local village folk who had also gathered. Our visitors filled the large semi-circular platform facing the congregation. The service began with the singing of the twenty-third Psalm and prayer. Then, when the District Officer had spoken on behalf of the visitors, the Ata presented the Discharge Cards. All eyes were focussed on him, as this was the first occasion when an Ata "looked upon the leper" – a sight strictly forbidden to his forefathers. After the dedicatory prayer, Mr. Dickson gave a short message, explaining so clearly how those returning to their home could best show their thankfulness to God by faith in Jesus Christ and love for their fellow-sufferers all over this Igala land.

'Some of our European visitors found it difficult to appreciate that the 300 patients were those facing them in the congregation! Such cheerfulness and hope were revealed in their faces that our visitors could not reconcile this with their former ideas concerning leprosy. What has made such a difference? The new drug certainly has been most effective, but I would add, without hesitation, that the Gospel message, and the prayers of many, have brought a hope and cheer which are eternal.

'The following day, Sunday, we had special services and an opportunity of giving final words of instruction to those who were leaving. One of the women had prepared several basins full of rice, fish, etc. to distribute amongst the patients she was leaving behind. These friends of hers later gathered their pennies and half-pennies together and gave her seven shillings and ninepence. This she brought at the close of the afternoon service as her thanksgiving to God, because in this Settlement she had found salvation and healing.'

One significant incident, not recorded by the doctor, was vividly recalled by others who were present when this woman came to the Holleys' house to say her final goodbye. She found Marion on the verandah with one-year-old Alison. Instinctively the woman reached out to embrace the little girl. But would a caring mother entrust her precious child to someone who had suffered from leprosy? For only a second Mrs. Holley hesitated. Then, with a smile, she placed Alison in those eager arms. The onlookers gasped. Now their last lingering doubt was gone. The doctor and his wife must surely believe that the discharged patients were really 'clean'. Leprosy could be cured!

CHAPTER FOUR

When God is in it

FURLOUGH WAS no time of idleness for Bill Holley.
He was a gifted speaker, often invited to take part in conferences, meetings and church services. His greatest
satisfaction, however, came in telling of how God was at
work in Igala.

'It was our joy to discharge thirty-one symptom-free
patients last year,' he reported in 1953. 'Most of these
have a definite knowledge of Jesus Christ as their
Saviour. One man has begun work as a colporteur,
selling books and witnessing to people in their own
homes. Two of the women are now helping in our
children's home. Some have settled with their
families in Ochadamu village, in order to be within
reach of the Christian fellowship that has come to
mean so much to them.

'The settlement has been growing steadily from
110 patients two years ago to 530 today. We now
have a church, a temporary hospital and a home for
babies whose mothers are patients. A small school is
going up at the present time. It will give us two class-
rooms for the forty children who have leprosy. But
these are only mud buildings. They won't last long.
What we need is a builder, someone who could or-

ganise the making of bricks and the erection of permanent wards and school-rooms. Will you join us in praying that God may send someone like that? Oh, and it would be even better if he could have a wife who is a nurse!'

Imagine Dr. Holley's delight to hear soon afterwards that a young builder had offered his services to the Mission – and his wife was a nurse! Mervyn and Florence Crooks were not the only ones whom the Lord of the harvest directed to Nigeria, and elsewhere, through the deputation ministry of Bill Holley. His enthusiasm and compassion were infectious. Above all, he radiated confidence in a great God who was able to meet the most intimate needs of those who put their trust in Him.

One instance of this provision that he loved to share concerned a twelve-year-old boy.

'He was not a heavy bundle,' Dr. Holley recalled. 'His body was thin, his legs completely paralysed and his face emaciated. But his sunken eyes were bright with expectant hope that he would be healed. He was suffering from advanced tuberculosis of the spine and had been ill for many months. About a year previously he had been to a Government hospital, but after two months there his people had carried him back home, where native doctors had already tried their best with no success. Then someone told them of the Mission dispensary and his brother carried him about twelve miles to Ochadamu.

'Humanly speaking, it seemed hopeless, but we felt we couldn't turn the boy away. After all, many folk were praying that God would manifest His power in cases just like this, so he was brought into one of the little mud houses. His brother agreed to stay and supply his food, while we treated his sickness. That evening we explained that his disease was very advanced, but that the God in whom we trusted was a Great Physician. We knelt in prayer, asking God to guide us in the treatment so that he might walk again.

'Then something very wonderful happened. Within forty-eight hours we had a visit from the chemist who had been supplying our drugs. He had travelled almost three hundred miles and this was the first and only occasion on which he visited Ochadamu during our two and a half years there. He spent about an hour with us. Just as he was leaving, he offered us samples of a new drug which was being used in the treatment of tuberculosis – a drug which, until that time, had not been used in Nigeria. We told him about our young patient and he gave us all the samples he possessed, so treatment began that very evening.

'Momo was convinced of improvement from the first injection, and after a few weeks he began to have movement in his feet and then in his legs. Each evening, as our dispensary boy gathered the patients and their friends to hear the Word of God, Momo listened eagerly. One of our houseboys was specially interested because he, too, had suffered from a T.B. spine and the Lord had healed him at Etinan hospital a few years previously. Almost daily he visited Momo, encouraging him and telling him about the One whom he himself was trusting and who was able to heal both body and soul.

'Gradually Momo began to understand God's way of salvation, and some three months later when the day came for him to journey home with his brother, they both realised that Jesus was not only the Great Physician, but also their Saviour. What a joy it was to see this little lad walk down the road! Soon afterwards, he returned to give thanks, and to let us know that he had started school again.'

Dr. and Mrs. Kearney had been in charge at Ochadamu during the Holley's furlough but now it was time for them to retire, leaving Bill as the only Mission doctor in Igala. Appeals for more missionaries had so far fallen on deaf ears but Igala helpers were being raised up, some of whom were themselves suffering from leprosy.

It was in January 1952 that Dr. Holley first met John Atabo and encouraged him to come to Ochadamu for treatment. The doctor was an excellent judge of character and saw great potential in his young patient. He was given the job of teaching the children in the little schoolroom and, in 1954, was employed as interpreter and general assistant. He was amazed at the many and varied tasks undertaken so cheerfully by Dr. Holley. Whether in supervising workers or keeping accounts, negotiating with suppliers and officials, conducting the huge clinics or sharing the gospel, John was constantly learning lessons that would prepare him for responsibilities in coming years. It wasn't all work, however. Bill Holley still loved a game of football and was always regarded as a formidable opponent!

Sometimes, when other duties permitted, the doctor and his helpers would pack a few basic medicines and set out for distant places in Igala or across the Benue river to the Bassa people. On these treks there often were no proper roads or accommodation. After a hard day's cycling or walking, they would lie down to rest for the night under an open sky. Whatever the circumstances Dr. Holley was full of enthusiasm, rejoicing especially when they discovered little groups of new believers, drawn together through the influence of former patients.

One of these was a young girl who had first been contacted by Elder Matthew. Out on his bicycle one day he had seen her sweeping the native doctor's compound. He noticed that she had a patch of leprosy on her body and that half of a finger was missing. Calling her over he said:

'There's a white man at Ochadamu who has strong medicine for that sickness.'

The girl was really annoyed with him and said:

'I'm doing what my people have always done. They have brought the sacrifice and this doctor is treating me.'

The godly old man went on his way, but the seed had been sown in her heart. She could see that her leprosy was becoming worse rather than better, so before long she arrived at Ochadamu. As her body responded to treatment, Aluda's heart opened to receive the Saviour, and when the time came for discharge she went home with her Igala New Testament and hymnbook.

About three months later, the chief of her village came to Ochadamu.

'I'm not coming to get medicine,' he announced. 'I want you to send us a teacher.'

'What makes you want a teacher?' asked Dr. Holley.

'Well,' he replied, 'you know that girl from our village who had leprosy? When she came home she began to gather the people together when they came back from their farms. She lights the lamp and teaches us hymns and reads God's Word. Now we want our children to be taught this good Word.'

Always eager to respond to such a request, Bill Holley called the Ochadamu people together, told them about the need and asked:

'Could we not send Joshua?'

Now Joshua was one of the patients soon to be discharged. When he came to the settlement many months before, he had said firmly:

'I'll come for the medicine but I don't want your message.'

'Fair enough,' agreed the doctor, so Joshua came in and began treatment.

At first he was nowhere to be seen when evening prayers were conducted. Then his face appeared on the fringe of the circle of light. Then he moved a little nearer, until he was at the front and asking very difficult questions. Eventually he received the Saviour and became a real witness to his fellow-patients.

Joshua was keen to serve the Lord so he was sent to Aluda's village, with the promise of six pounds a month from Ochadamu. The village people gave him a little house and a piece of land to farm.

He was told:

'You can farm in the mornings, teach the children in the afternoons and gather the people in the evenings to hear the Word of God.'

Teaching began in a very simple way. At first Joshua drew the letters of the alphabet in the sand; then he got a blackboard. But although equipment was meagre, the young teacher had the most important qualification – a personal relationship with Jesus Christ and a deep desire to share Him with others. Twenty-five years later Bill Holley would meet him and Aluda again, still faithfully serving the Lord. As Bill loved to say:

'Little is much when God is in it.'

CHAPTER FIVE

Relationships

ALTHOUGH FAR away from his native land, Bill Holley still retained a deep concern for his family and friends, especially his youngest brother. When Cecil first went to work in Belfast, Bill warned him against following his early example in that city of bright lights and subtle temptations. 'You need the Lord,' he would say with an encouraging hand on the shoulder. But he was too wise to spoil their relationship with frequent preaching. One day the opportunity would come. Meantime, secret prayer was the safest and surest resource.

In 1953, Bill was on furlough in Portstewart. Cecil was there too for the Bank holiday week-end. On Sunday he went to hear his brother preach in a nearby church. The sermon was on Naaman and as sin was likened to the disease of leprosy Cecil became distinctly uneasy. That evening Bill was preaching again, this time about the three people of different ages whom Jesus raised from the dead. After describing them he went on to warn his hearers:

'If you are without Christ you, too, are dead, spiritually dead, no matter what age you may be.'

Later, the two brothers went for a walk on the golf course beside their father's home. 'Cecil,' said Bill, 'would you like to be a Christian?' It was God's time. There on the green grass, within sound of the waves breaking on the golden sand, they knelt together in prayer, and another member of the Holley family found new life in Christ.

There was great excitement at Ochadamu in March 1955 when news filtered through that Bill and Marion's third child had been born in Enugu. Guns were fired into the air and everyone rejoiced that at last the doctor had a son!

Five months later the mood changed as little Martin had to be rushed back to the Government hospital for emergency surgery. In their haste, the anxious parents took time to glance at the promise for that day on the Scripture calendar. It read: *'The Lord hath need of him!'* Did this mean that Martin was to be taken home to heaven then? Or did it foretell a lifetime of usefulness in God's service? Either way the familiar words brought reassurance that the Lord was in control and would work out His perfect plan.

All went well with the operation, but there were fears that the obstruction might recur and the Holleys were advised to get their little boy home to U.K. as soon as possible. Sadly, but with the peace of a right decision, Marion set out with four-year-old Alison and a sickly six-months-old Martin.

This was not the first painful separation for the family, for at five years of age Rosemary had been left with her grandparents to go to school in Portstewart. Now, unexpectedly, she was joined by her mother, sister and new baby brother, leaving a lonely father in Igala to get on with the work to which God had called him.

It was a great blessing that he had the company of the Crooks family who by now were settled at Ochadamu. In addition to looking after their two small boys, Florence

34

was able to take on Marion's duties in the baby clinic. Under Mervyn's skilled guidance the new hospital made swift progress – a foretaste of many fine buildings which were to be his lasting contribution to medical and educational work in Igala.

In due course, Dr. Esther Davis relieved Dr. Holley for home leave, and the Holley family enjoyed some refreshing months together in Portstewart. The time had come when Alison, also, must begin her schooling, so the return to Igala in 1957 meant saying goodby to two little girls. There was, however, something special to look forward to at Ochadamu. For years they had been longing for a qualified Matron to give leadership and training to the faithful but untrained helpers who, so far, had been the only nursing staff. Norah Curran was a Scottish nurse, called to Nigeria through a contact with the Dicksons. She had begun work at Ochadamu and was now looking forward, rather nervously, to meeting Bill Holley about whom she had heard such glowing reports. She vividly remembers her first day with him in theatre:

'He turned from "scrubbing up" and went pale when he saw the patient swathed in lint bandages. I was soon enlightened as to the need for economy! Then we both enjoyed a good laugh and all my fears vanished.'

She soon observed the doctor's boundless energy and dedication:

'During his coffee break he would be seen tearing around on his bike, checking up on patients at work, supervising activities, and showing real concern over even minor injuries. Patients were made aware that work was for their benefit and to provide better accommodation, water supply, etc., but I don't ever remember him asking anyone to do anything that he was not prepared to do himself. He gave God all the glory and encouraged others to do the same.'

One aspect of Bill Holley's life that made a deep impression on his fellow workers concerned his family relationships.

'I cannot think of Bill without Marion – they were ONE,' Norah recalls. 'Even after the simplest meal there was a gracious word of thanks, setting an example to little Martin who would then say, "That was 'licious. Thank you for a lovely dinner."'

Such harmony inside and outside the home was not maintained without constant vigilance. As well as his commitments at Ochadamu, Bill had growing responsibilities as a member of the Mission's Field Executive and in the Qua Iboe Church. Sundays usually found him preaching, sometimes in tiny village churches, sometimes to congregations of over a thousand people. All this was good, but when it came after a night broken by medical emergencies, the first thing to suffer was the doctor's early morning tryst with God. Before long the effects began to show in daily life. Small things loomed large and the customary good humour gave way to irritability and impatience. But Bill Holley was sensitive to the still, small voice of the Holy Spirit. Recognising what was happening he sought forgiveness and resolved that, however pressing other demands might be, the precious hour of devotion and intercession must never again be neglected.

Looking back Marion recalls:

'The Lord helped him to make this a No. 1 priority and those who knew him best realised that this was the secret of his infectious Christianity. I used to tell him that he was the best visual aid I had of a true follower of Christ!'

By now Martin was a lively little boy, up to all sorts of mischief and a source of amusement and delight to patients and staff alike. At fourteen months when home

36

on furlough he had had another mishap and sustained a fractured skull. Happily there were no complications and he was soon back in Nigeria playing with his Igala friends and the Crooks boys, Roger and Stephen.

As time went on, much prayerful thought was given to Martin's education. Rosemary and Alison had been very happy with the maternal grandparents, but Mr. Jenks died in 1958 and, although their grandmother was willing to care for Martin also, it seemed a lot for her to cope with three children single-handed. In the event, the decision was made for them when Marion became ill with thyroid trouble which needed long-term medication. No doctor was available to relieve Bill at Ochadamu, so, after earnest prayer and heart-searching, they felt that for the sake of the work the family should separate once more, mother and children living in Portstewart while the father remained in Igala. Mrs. Holley described their two-and-a-half year separation as:

'A testing time, but we clung on in faith to what we felt sure was God's way for us and He gave the needed grace to each of us while we were apart from each other.'

Ochadamu Medical Centre was continuing to grow in medical and spiritual effectiveness. It was a regular occurrence for men, women and children to profess faith in Christ before the assembled congregation on Sunday mornings. The doctor never forgot one small boy who made his way to the front after the service. When asked why he wanted to trust the Lord, he replied:

'Because we have been singing, "I'm not too young to come to Jesus for He loves a little child."'

Such incidents made all the hard work and separations worthwhile.

Over 3,000 patients were now under treatment for leprosy in residential care, segregation villages and clinics. Another 13,000 attended the general dispensary each year, and around 1,500 mothers were receiving help at the ante-natal clinic. There was great need, however, for a place where their babies could be safely delivered and this was met by the completion of the Hilda Dickson Maternity Unit in November 1959. The opening ceremony, performed by Mrs. Dickson's niece, Dr. Alice Davis, was attended by a great crowd of people, including the Ata of Igala and his counsellors. The only disappointment was that Marion could not be present to share her husband's joy in another fulfilled vision.

A tragic event which the doctor also had to face without her help occurred in 1961 when a lorry full of women travelling to their conference at Ochadamu got out of control on a hill leading to the river at Ogbulu. The lorry plunged into the water and overturned. When Dr. Holley arrived on the scene the bodies of seven young women and two one-year-old babies had been recovered. Many more were still pinned under the lorry, some with serious injuries. It was assumed that the conference should be cancelled but the Christian women said, 'No! The devil wants to stop us but we need to meet with God.' Faith had triumphed over tragedy.

After two years on his own at Ochadamu, the time came for Dr. Holley to join his family in Ireland, a decision made easier by an offer from Dr. and Mrs. Kearney to return for a short period. By now Robert Thompson, loyally assisted by John Atabo, was well able to cope with management responsibilities and Ann Roxburgh was proving her worth on the nursing staff. On the home front, it was clear that Marion's health would not allow her to return to Nigeria and the children were at an age when they needed both parents. Everything pointed to the fact that, after fourteen years, Bill's overseas commission was drawing to a close.

As news leaked out that the doctor might not be returning after furlough there was great lamentation at Ochadamu and throughout Igala. On 12th October 1961, staff, patients, missionaries and other friends gathered for an emotional 'send-off'. Tributes and gifts poured in, official addresses and touching letters from individuals whom Bill Holley had helped physically, spiritually and materially. Only the assurance of being in the will of God carried him through the sad farewells. He knew that his Nigerian friends understood his decision for they, too, realised the importance of family life. One thing was sure, they would have a continuing place in his affection and prayers, and, God willing, he would return some day to visit them again.

CHAPTER SIX

The Man was the Message

BILL HOLLEY was never a man for looking back. Indeed one of his favourite quotations was: 'Don't dig up in unbelief what you've sown in faith.' So, confident that the God who called him to Nigeria had now called him back to his place of birth, he waited in faith to see what further service lay ahead. He had not long to wait.

In 1962, after six months as a senior medical officer in the Route Hospital in Ballymoney, he was appointed assistant to Dr. William Burns in general practice in Coleraine. A year later he became a partner, working with Dr. Burns in Coleraine Health Centre until 1974.

This was a specially happy period of family life in the first home they could really call their own. Each child in turn confessed faith in Christ, and after a gap of seven years another little girl, Patricia, was born in August 1962 – the first of the four to have a British Birth Certificate.

Bill quickly became involved with Christian activities in his home town and throughout the province. Portstewart Convention had played an important part in his call to Nigeria and in 1961 he was invited to become a member of its interdenominational committee. Living so near to Portstewart enabled him to assist in many practical ways. He knew how essential it was for missionaries on furlough to be physically and spiritually refreshed and he gladly undertook responsibility for operating a Hospitality Fund, making it easier for many of them to enjoy the full week's ministry. However, the Convention's Chairman, Rev. Dr. W.M. Craig, considered that Dr. Holley's greatest contribution was 'the consistent fragrance and influence of his life, embodying the truths that were proclaimed from the platform. His smile was genuine, his eyes were sincere, his handshake was firm and his countenance radiated the joy of the Lord with whom he walked.'

As a family doctor Bill Holley brought to his patients in Coleraine the same Christ-like caring that he had shown in Nigeria. Not only was he an excellent physician but a wise counsellor and a man of action. On one memorable occasion, his timely intervention prevented a four-year-old boy being sent to a school for retarded children, an assessment that was dramatically vindicated when the same boy eventually qualified as a barrister and became Crown Prosecutor in an English Court.

Monday, 9th November, 1970, was a date Bill never forgot because that was the day when Arthur Williams first came into his home. Arthur was a young man of twenty-eight years of age with a serious drink problem. Although he had seen the terrible effects of alcohol on his father, his own will had not been strong enough to resist its power. At sixteen years of age he had become drunk for the first time. By now it was a continuous condition, robbing him of livelihood, friends and self-respect. A few days previously he had acknowledged at last that he was in need of help and his mother arranged for him to see their doctor whom she had known since school days. It was destined in the will of God to be a momentous visit.

There was a warmth about Bill Holley that disarmed the young man and he found himself pouring out all his heart-break. To his surprise there was no lecture, no hasty judgement. Instead, this doctor, dark eyes aglow with the love of his Master, said:

'Arthur, I'll give you some treatment, but what you really need is Jesus Christ. He's a living Saviour. He can forgive your sin and give you power to overcome this thing that's killing you.'

Recalling that first meeting, Arthur Williams says:

'The man was the message. Jesus Christ was shining through Bill Holley. Hope was kindled in my heart that day. I rolled up the prescription he'd given me and said, "I'll take Jesus!"'

Patiently and winsomely the doctor explained the way of salvation and shared the promises of God through which he himself had found peace in believing. Together they knelt in prayer, and a desperately needy young man received Christ as his Saviour and Lord.

That was just the beginning. The demon drink does not easily release its victims and for six months fought to retain control of spirit, mind and body. Dr. Holley was on call at all hours of day and night to help deal with the recurring crises. He himself was very aware of having to live close to God in order to have the spiritual resources for this battle and Arthur remembers him remarking with typical humour:

'You know, Arthur, I believe the Lord sent you along to keep me from middle-aged back-sliding!'

Other people with drink problems had come for help and a group of ten or more began to meet every week in the Holley home. They, too, experienced the same compassionate care and understanding from both Bill and Marion. Society might treat them as worthless but here each one was made to feel special, and precious in the sight of God.

It was the middle of 1971 before Arthur Williams finally found deliverance. He knew now that *he* couldn't live the Christian life, only Christ could do that through the indwelling Holy Spirit. His part was to trust and obey. By this time his wife had become a Christian and together they began a new life of service to God.

After a year's Bible Training at Cliff College in Derbyshire and a year as Lay Evangelist with the Methodist Church in Ireland, Arthur was called to be Pastor of the Findlay Memorial Church in Glasgow. Incidentally, this church had an interesting link with Qua Iboe, having presented a Shield to be awarded annually to the best Sunday School in the Qua Iboe Church. During his six years in Glasgow, Pastor Williams was used by God to lead many who were addicted to drugs and alcohol to faith in Christ. When Dr. Holley went to preside at a meeting there, they were introduced as his 'spiritual grandchildren!'

Meantime in Coleraine, and later in Portstewart, the group now known as Alcoholics Victorious was continuing to grow. There were three activities in its weekly meetings – sharing of each other's problems, failures and successes; study of the Word of God, and Prayer. One by one its members met the Saviour and in turn many of them went out to help others. A similar pattern was followed in the *Stauros Foundation which Arthur Williams was led to establish in 1980, and which ten years later had six full-time workers in Scotland, England, Ireland and the Isle of Man. Though not officially involved with this Trust, Bill Holley was always regarded as its father figure, whose advice and prayers were greatly valued.

* Stauros is the Greek word for Cross.

Having seen the devastating effects of alcohol in so many lives and homes, Bill never understood how any Christian could condone its use. He was often invited to speak to young people in school or youth groups about its dangers but his message was never negative. He saw alcohol, like drugs, as a poor substitute for God's good gift of the Holy Spirit, often quoting Paul's guidance to the church at Ephesus, *'Be not drunk with wine, wherein is excess, but be filled with the Spirit.'*

Reality was Bill Holley's passion. As a young man he had tried the substitutes and found them to fail. Now he wanted to help others to avoid the same mistakes.

CHAPTER SEVEN

A Foretaste of Heaven

The Immigration Officer at Lagos International Airport gazed in unbelief, first at the passport in his hand and then at its owner. It was hard to reconcile the date of birth, 2nd June 1917, with the youthful appearance of the handsome man standing before him.

'Holley,' he exclaimed, 'you are an old man!'

Bill Holley chuckled. It was great to be back in Nigeria!

Twenty years had passed since he had last set foot on African soil. Those years had brought many new interests and responsibilities, but his Nigerian friends had never been far from his thoughts and prayers. He had maintained close links with the Qua Iboe Mission, now known as the Qua Iboe Fellowship, and, in 1974, had been appointed a member of its Home Council. Four years later he became its chairman, an office to which he brought a wealth of experience, not only as a former missionary, but as a member of the Advisory Committee which, in 1959, had initiated the handing over of institutions and property from Mission to Church control.

Council members remember the helpful way in which he led the opening devotional exercises and guided its business. But his chief delight was to interview and accept new missionaries. He never lost his sense of wonder at the grace of God in saving, calling and equipping young men and women for His service. The day after the Council meeting, he would be on the 'phone with the General Secretary, Rev. Bill Leach, to talk over decisions that had been made and to confirm his thoughts on what had been discussed. His was no superficial interest. This was God's work. It must be done in God's way and for God's glory.

Now, on 11th July 1981, at the invitation of the Qua Iboe Church, Bill Holley had returned to see the fruits of that work and to join in celebrating the Golden Jubilee of the Church in Igala.

The last two decades had brought immense changes to Nigeria. Driving through the streets of Lagos he was utterly amazed at the thronging traffic and noisy comments of the drivers, the magnificent roads, bridges and public buildings, and the throbbing vitality of a largely youthful population. Best of all was the warm welcome from the godly pastor and elders from one of the Lagos churches, who committed him and his fellow-traveller, Bill Leach, to God's care and blessing for their coming ministry.

Before going north the visitors spent six days in the Qua Iboe area where both had begun their missionary service. John Atabo had travelled down from Igala to greet Bill on his arrival at the Samuel Bill Theological College. It was a heart-warming reunion and soon they were seated on the steps of the verandah, looking excitedly at photographs Bill had brought out and reminiscing about their happy days working together at Ochadamu. Next morning John was off again in his little Peugeot Pick-up to get ready for the visitors in Igala.

The six days at S.B.T.C. passed quickly, with many old friends to greet and new developments to see. One night an incident occurred which took Bill Holley right back to his time at Etinan hospital. A message came to say that a woman was seriously ill in a village three miles away. Without hesitation, he set out to help her, delighted to be a missionary doctor once again!

The Annual Prize-giving at S.B.T.C. was on 15th July and Dr. Holley had been invited to take part. As he rose to address the assembled students, his heart was filled with thanksgiving for all that he had heard of their testimonies, and for the gifted tutors whom God had raised up to train them as pastors, preachers, teachers and missionaries. Looking over the crowd of expectant faces before him he said:

'I can think of no better introduction to our Nigerian visit than this Bible College Prize-giving, for surely it is the Bible and its message which unites us in Christ Jesus.'

He went on to speak about that transforming book as the *Word of God* in which He reveals His will to man; as the *Bread of Life* to nourish our spiritual lives; as the *Sword of the Spirit* by which we conquer Satan; as the *Hammer* which breaks down resistance in sinful hearts; as the *Light* which penetrates the darkness.

'This Book is alive,' he said. 'It is different from every other book in the world. *Know* it in your head, *stow* it in your heart, *show* it in your life, *sow* it in the world; and may you know the anointing and enabling of the Holy Spirit.'

Early next morning the visitors set off by car, eager to get up to what Bill called 'the wide open spaces of Igala'. Every stage of the journey brought memories and surprises, culminating in a tremendous welcome at Ochadamu.

All evening the visitors kept coming. At 8 p.m. prayers were led by Elder Solomon Adaudu, who had been discharged as a patient in 1961 and was now the Centre's Evangelist. That night Bill wrote in his diary:

47

'Great thrill to hear him read Luke 15 verses 8-10 and speak of joy because of our coming, and then preach on the lost who were found.'

Sunday, 19th July, brought the special Remembrance Service at Ugwolawo, attended by well over 1,000 people, including Senators and members of the House of Representatives. The highlight came when the chairman asked if anyone there had been present when the first baptisms had taken place in 1934. As three elderly men stood up, Bill Holley's thoughts went back to the story of how six pagan men had gone to search for the 'living water' which they heard was obtainable across the Niger. They had returned with pots full of water, which the people then began to worship in their longing for something to satisfy their spiritual thirst. Soon afterwards, the first Qua Iboe missionary, David O'Neill, arrived with the life-giving message of the gospel. Every day for six months one young man had walked seventeen miles to listen to that message. Matthew's heart was opened to receive the Saviour and he became the very first Igala elder. In time, each one of those six men, and many others, found salvation and satisfaction in Jesus Christ. What a joy it was to celebrate the fiftieth anniversary of those significant events and to renew fellowship with so many old friends that day at Ugwolawo!

Dr. Holley's companions have vivid recollections of those days in Igala – of his delight at spotting familiar faces; of the rapturous embraces; of the visits to lovely Christian families and the special buns baked in his honour! Bill's diary, written for Marion who was caring for her mother at home, gives an insight into his reactions. From it we give a few typical extracts:

'*21st July.* Ochaja. Crowds inside and outside the church, more than 800 present. What a change from grass walls and roof of first church! Electric fans now!

So, so many faces I know, some of former patients. Oh! the thrill of seeing them among God's people after twenty years!'

'22nd July. Palm oil chop this evening. Delicious! The event of today was meeting Daniel Negedu (one-time helper at Ochadamu dispensary) and his wife Grace. I saw him at Ankpa hospital where he is Senior Nursing Superintendent. Great thrill to meet the same quiet Daniel. He showed me through the hospital and then to his house to meet Grace. *So* encouraging after twenty years!'

'26th July. Joshua, John Atabo and Solomon called this evening, three former patients, now serving the Lord in different places. We prayed together. Great thrill to have a share in this work. At least twenty ex-patients have gone out as evangelists since 1950. Late tonight, news that Solomon had spoken to a girl of fourteen admitted to the dispensary – attempted suicide. He led her to the Lord and peace. Praise the Lord! Wondrous grace!'

'28th July. En route to Bassa stayed overnight with Robert and Joyce Hyslop (independent missionaries). Warm welcome. Talked till midnight. Robert told a lovely story of an old Bassa woman called Mary, who was treated and converted at Ochadamu. She died at home. She was ready to go and requested only that in heaven her house would be beside Dr. Holley who led her to Christ, David Gilmore who helped her to live for Christ, and Robert Hyslop who helped her to die in Christ. At her burial the Christians rejoiced that another one had been safely gathered HOME.'

'1st August. Igala Jubilee. Drove to Idah from Ochadamu, arriving 8 a.m. Crowds gathered in the church compound. Thirty pastors and elders from

the South – a very good representation. By bus to the Ata's Palace and waited on His Highness. The Ata signed a cheque for the Qua Iboe Church and was very commending in his speech. Bill Leach handed over a photo of the Ata's father and we all received Kola nuts and returned to the church compound. Heard today of two babies born at Ochadamu who are now training in medicine!'

The time had come to say farewell once more to Ochadamu and to Igala. On the way to the airport the travellers visited the flourishing Qua Iboe Churches in the northern cities of Makurdi, Jos, Kaduna, Zaria and Kano. At Kaduna about 200 young people gathered in the church to meet them that morning. For two hours they plied the visitors with questions, turning up the relevant places already marked in their Bibles. Some of the questions were very difficult and Bill was quick to pass them on to his theologically-trained companions, Bill Leach and David Smith who had joined them from S.B.T.C. He had a hearty laugh when he was introduced as Rev. Dr. Bill Holley! That was not his calling, but he did recognise the great need and opportunity for a high standard of Bible-based ministry among these educated young people who would be future leaders in church and community. One of his diary entries stressed this:

'Reminded of the Date Palm tree. The roots must go twelve feet down before the first leaves appear. We need experienced men from Nigeria and U.K. – *"Pray the Lord the harvest ..."*'

It had been an exceedingly busy month. Dr. Holley had spoken at thirty-four meetings in twenty-three days, not to mention almost four days of Executive and committee meetings and many personal interviews. He was coming home with new burdens for prayer and action, and a host of memories to share with Marion. There was just one regret:

'If only you had been there,' he said. 'Being back in Nigeria was a lovely bonus from the Lord – a little foretaste of heaven!'

CHAPTER EIGHT

Freedom Behind Bars

All through his life Bill Holley was keenly aware of the sovereign hand of God opening and closing doors of opportunity before him. One such redirection had taken place early in 1978. After fourteen busy and happy years in general practice, Bill's health was beginning to give cause for concern and he realised the need to reduce his work-load. As the door to general practice closed, another opened into a completely new sphere of service. On the 1st of March he took up duty as Senior Medical Officer in H.M. Prison at Magilligan on the shores of Lough Foyle, not far from Londonderry.

What became known as the 'Troubles' had been in progress in Northern Ireland since 1969 and prisoners from both republican and loyalist sides of the strife-torn community were being held at Magilligan. Although he had served as a Police Surgeon for ten years, it was a new experience for Bill Holley to plunge into the tensions and problems of prison life. As he treated physical and psychological maladies, many of them self-inflicted, his heart went out to these men who were caught up in a never-ending spiral of bitterness and violence. If only they could meet the Saviour! But how?

As always his chief resource was prayer. A number of

other Christians were employed in the prison and the doctor began to gather them together every week in his office to pray for prisoners in their care and for opportunities to witness for Christ. At first results seemed slow but right from the start a good foundation was being laid for the coming days.

Prison Fellowship, an organisation founded in the United States by former Congressman Charles Colson, had begun to operate in Northern Ireland, with Dr. Holley as a member of its Board of Trustees. In May 1981, James McIlroy was appointed as its first Director. He already knew Bill Holley and relied greatly on his advice and support. By now the doctor was respected and trusted by the Prison Governor and through his good offices a meeting was convened with the four official Prison Chaplains. As a result, permission was granted to begin a weekly 'Sing-along', to which all prisoners were invited, irrespective of their political or religious affiliations.

'What a wonderful time we had each Thursday evening at these gatherings.' James McIlroy recalls. 'After a few initial restraints, republicans and loyalists shared their hymn-sheets and sang heartily together. They listened attentively to the short challenging talks and, as time progressed, we saw friendships formed where there was enmity before.'

This was the developing situation to which Bill Holley returned after his visit to Nigeria. The following year brought him many opportunities for ministry at Qua Iboe Fellowship Conferences and also at larger gatherings in Northern Ireland and further afield. Happily, some of his addresses were captured on tape, among them one recorded on the 31st October, 1982, when he was the principal speaker at a Festival of Male Voice Praise in Larne, Co. Antrim. It was his 35th wedding anniversary, and just over forty years since he had become a Christian. He was in reminiscent mood, but much of what he said concerned more recent happenings. The story which follows is taken from that memorable address.

After three-and-a-half years of patient prayer, events had begun to move at Magilligan Prison. In December 1981, rioting in another prison had made it necessary to transfer some long-term prisoners to Magilligan. The night after their arrival some of them turned up at the Prison Fellowship meeting and, to his surprise, Dr. Holley noticed that they had copies of *Good News for Modern Man*.

The next morning he sought one of them out in his cell and sat down beside him on the bunk bed.

*'Michael,' he said, 'I see you have a Bible – do you read it?'

'I do,' replied Michael.

'Why?' was the next question.

'Because I'm a Christian.'

Bill Holley could hardly believe his ears. He knew this man to be a member of the notorious I.N.L.A. – a Marxist, who for eighteen months had been on what was known as the 'dirty protest'. This man – a Christian!

'Tell me about it,' he invited.

'Well,' explained Michael, 'there was only one book in the cell. It was a Bible. I read it from cover to cover but it made no sense. One Sunday at Mass, I said to the priest, "Have you any good books about the Bible?"

"No need for other books," replied the priest. "Go back and read John's Gospel and ask the Holy Spirit to speak to you."

'I did that,' continued Michael. 'Jesus became alive to

---

* The names of prisoners have been changed.

me and I got all churned up inside. The other prisoners heard that two more members of the security forces had been killed and they began to cheer. But I couldn't cheer. Then one night on my bed as I was going off to sleep …. but you'll not believe me?'

He looked at the doctor with a question in his eyes.

'Go on,' said Bill.

'Well,' he said, 'that night, that filthy cell was filled with a Presence. A voice said to me, "Michael, trust in Jesus." I said, 'I will!" – and I did.'

Michael had become a new creation in Christ Jesus.

It was with a full heart that Bill Holley left Magilligan for home that evening. Next day Michael greeted him with a piece of paper in his hand. On it were the names of fourteen prisoners.

'Doc,' he said, 'would you teach us the Bible?'

Bill gladly agreed to discuss it with the Governor, and not only he, but all the chaplains gave their approval. Eighteen men turned up for 'Doc's Bible class' at 2.30 p.m. on the first Monday in January 1982. Some were tattooed with loyalist slogans, others displayed the republican colours, but all wanted to know about the Word of God.

Now, ten months later, their number had risen to thirty, and they had just completed the study of John's Gospel. One of the members of the Bible Class was *Sean. He had been on hunger strike for 56 days in 1981. For the last four days he had been blind and extremely weak but still refused medical help. Then his mother said that as soon as he became unconcious she would call for the doctor and, knowing that he would not be allowed to die, Sean agreed to take some food. When he was brought to Magilligan he was still unable to walk, but he had found a new purpose in living.

As Bill Holley stood before the packed congregation

in Larne on that October evening he took an envelope from his pocket and said:

'Let me read you part of a letter that Sean has written to me:

"Before leaving Long Kesh I wrote a letter of resignation to the I.N.L.A. As I left I felt a cloud lifting from me. I suffered there and almost died, but out of it all God came into my life and I'm a better person for it. I've discovered a beauty in life I never knew existed. I've found a depth in life that I was unaware of; I found a love beyond comparison in gentleness, purity and truth. I have found fulfilment. I have found eternal life. Pray God I may never let them go for the material things and cares of this world. Knowing Jesus has brought me freedom, freedom from hatred, from selfishness, from bitterness, from lust – freedom of spirit. Although I'm still bound physically behind locked doors and gates, I am free, for freedom of mind is freedom indeed."'

There were few dry eyes as Bill Holley folded the letter and concluded:

'That's what God is doing in our prisons today. Will you pray for us as we meet tomorrow and every Monday afternoon,' he appealed, 'and will you pray for those who have gone out into the community again, that they too might serve Christ and witness for Him?'

CHAPTER NINE

I Saw His Faith

On 20th May 1984, Marion's mother went to be with the Lord at the ripe old age of ninety-five years. Mrs. Jenks had lived with the Holleys for six years and, until latterly, enjoyed amazingly good health. Many tributes were paid to her Christian witness and example. Her grand-daughter, Alison, had come home from London for the funeral. As an experienced physio-therapist she was worried about her father's health and persuaded him to consult a neurologist. So it came to pass that, on his sixty-seventh birthday, Bill Holley was in a Belfast hospital awaiting the result of extensive tests. In God's goodness, Bill Leach was visiting him when the neurologist returned with the dreaded diagnosis – Motor Neurone Disease.

The seriousness of this condition was explained, but Bill did not need to be told. As a doctor he was only too well aware that there was no known cure, and no treatment to arrest the progressive degeneration of the nerves, with consequent weakness and wastage of muscles. For someone with Bill's zest for life it was a horrifying prospect. How could he face months, perhaps years of increasing disability and dependance? How could Marion and the family cope with it? What about those fellows at Magilligan and others who still needed help?

Such thoughts must have flashed before him in those first agonising moments. Then the habit of forty years took over and he turned his gaze to the One, who for the joy that was set before Him endured the cross.

'The future is in God's hands,' he said. 'I know I'm going to heaven.'

When the neurologist left, Bill Leach returned to that little room where time seemed to stand still. He remembers with awe the precious moments spent in fellowship and prayer, the mutual tears, and the parting embrace in the hospital corridor. A merciful heavenly Father had provided the sensitive human companionship needed in such an hour.

While he was still able, Bill went to say goodbye to his friends at Magilligan. It wasn't easy. A strong bond had been established between 'the Doc' and members of his Bible Class. In an interview with journalist Alf McCreary, 'Liam', a former member of the Provisional IRA, put it in his own words:

'I went to the Bible Study as a sort of joke. But the feeling there was much too real, there was a warmth in the place. I had to give respect where respect was due. That surprised me, giving that little bit of respect. I went a few times and I started to question myself. Outside the Bible Study I met Doc Holley during his normal rounds, and the interest and concern he had were outstanding. No one else in the system had that degree of concern for you. He was so well-placed, a man of authority, he had lots to do, lots of responsibilities, and yet he found time to stop and to find out if he could brighten your day. He would do anything for you, and you really believed his interest in you was genuine. You could see it, you could feel it.

'I made a commitment to Christ and I asked him to

take control of my whole life and to guide me. My cell-mate at that time was a Christian, so that was a great advantage. My former colleagues laughed at first. They thought I was joking, but then they realised I was serious and they became contemptuous. Even after my commitment, I questioned myself, but God kept me strong and kept me going ....
As well as this I was getting to know Doc Holley as time went on and he was *living* Christianity. Every day that we met you could see Christ, because of his genuine feeling and love for you. If you needed advice or guidance on the Word of God, Doc Holley would make sure that he had time to talk to you, even to go down to your cell and sit with you.

'He came to say "Goodbye" to us, because he knew what he had and he knew it was the last time he was coming in. It was "heavy", a few of us cried, and I remember thinking, "He's a man of God, he's worked for God all his life, why is God letting this happen to him now?" It took me quite some time to find solace in the Bible, but God told me that His ways are so much above our ways.'

By November Bill had lost the power of hands and arms. His speech and swallowing were affected and walking was increasingly difficult. The disease was developing rapidly. In a letter to the wide circle of friends who were praying for them, he and Marion shared their thoughts about Divine healing:

'As instructed in Scripture we called for the elders of the church who anointed Bill and prayed for his recovery in the will of God. We know God is able to heal and all our readings assure us that He is in control:

"Think it not strange concerning the fiery trial that is to try you ..." 1 Peter 4:12.

"He knoweth the way that I take. When He hath

59

tried me I shall come forth as gold ..." Job 23:10.
"My grace is sufficient for you ..." 2 Corinthians
12:9.
Also Psalm 138:8 and many such promises. We are
just learning to trust Him more fully – "The Author
and Finisher of our faith."

Every day we get new tokens of our Heavenly
Father's care; we have the strong support of a most
loving family and a caring church fellowship; hun-
dreds are praying for us, and so we leave the future
confidently with Him. We pray that the Prince of
Peace will rule in our lives continually and that His
purpose for us all will be fulfilled.'

During the next difficult months there were many
more remarkable tokens of the Lord's intimate understanding and infinite care. For a few weeks Bill managed
to communicate by using a simple mechanical aid. By
means of a bracket attached to his chin and slight move-
ments of his neck and head, he was able to tap out letters
on a small screen. Slowly, with great effort, words were
formed and sentences put together in an attempt to convey some of his thoughts.

'All the days of my life are recorded in Thy book,' he
wrote. And again, *'No future fears – just family tears.'*

Another sentence, painstakingly typed, revealed the
measure of his acceptance of God's will.

'I think this illness is an answer to my prayer –
"that I may know Him
and the power of his resurrection
and the fellowship of His sufferings."
(Philippians 3:10)'

It was wonderful that so many of the family were able
to be with Bill and Marion when they were most needed.
With perfect timing their eldest daughter, Rosemary

Kingston, arrived from Malawi, and Alison got six months' leave from her physio-therapy post in London. Martin and his wife had already moved from England to set up an optician's practice in Coleraine, where Patricia was nursing in the local hospital. All these brought much comfort and practical assistance, as did Bill's sister Anne and her husband, who lived nearby. His brother Cecil, with his wife and two sons were able to visit frequently being only an hour's journey away. Two other brothers and their children were in England and Canada.

An outstanding memory that the family will always cherish is the way that, even in extreme weakness, Bill maintained his daily quiet time with the Lord. The 'outward man' might be wasting away but the 'inner man' was being renewed day by day. As long as he could sit in a wheelchair, he was pushed to his desk where his Bible was propped up before him. Alongside it was a little blue notebook containing the names of those for whom he prayed regularly – family friends, Qua Iboe Church leaders, Ochadamu Medical Centre, missionaries working there and in various parts of the world, alcoholics, prisoners and others in special need. Who can tell how much was accomplished as the Holy Spirit made intercession through him in those days of seeming helplessness?

And there was still a ministry to his many visitors. As Bill's illness progressed there was growing concern among people whom he had befriended. They wanted to show their sympathy, to offer support; but sometimes they were reluctant to call. What could they say? What if they broke down?

'Liam' described his surprise at what he found:

'When I was out on parole and when I was released I went to visit Doc Holley. I saw his faith, it hadn't been shaken one iota by the disease he was suffering from. His family hadn't been shaken. His wife, Marion, was remarkable, and his son and daughters. That strengthened my faith and it made me determined to have a relationship with God that could sustain me to go through something as horrible as they had to go through.'

In later weeks only the movement of an eyebrow or the look in those expressive eyes could convey the response of a keenly alert mind. Undoubtedly there were bad days when everyone's spirits were low, but, even then, nothing could disturb the peace of God that was guarding heart and home. Marion recalls how, when night nursing became necessary, the Lord prompted three lovely Christian nurses to offer their services. She describes them as 'real ministering angels, as was an African Christian nursing sister from Malawi, studying at Coleraine university, who also offered help. It was moving to see her caring for him – a special token from the Lord in return for Bill's healing ministry in Africa.'

She was not the only African to bring comfort in those days. In Nigeria the Qua Iboe Church people had been shocked to hear of Dr. Holley's condition. There were many prayers for his recovery, but when it became clear that this was not God's will, two elders set out to greet their beloved missionary on behalf of all their people.

They arrived on Saturday 13th May, in time to join the annual Qua Iboe Fellowship conference in Portrush. Next day they were taken the four miles to the Holley home in Portstewart. As they entered his room, Bill's eyes overflowed at the sight of his good friends – Paul Achimugu, a prominent business man and son of Hon. Peter Achimugu, and Daniel Akwu, a leader in the field of education and in the Church. Although he was unable to speak, they sensed how glad he was to see them. They knew too how best to help him. Kneeling at his bedside they poured out their hearts in prayer, giving thanks for his Christlike life and praying that he might soon be released into the joy of the Lord's presence. Four weeks later that prayer was answered.

On 12th June 1985 a memorable service of thanksgiving was held in Portstewart Baptist Church where Bill was a dearly-loved elder. Representatives of the Qua Iboe Fellowship, Stauros Foundation and Prison Fellowship paid eloquent tribute to the grace of God in the life of His servant. As Bill would have wished, the dominant note was one of praise, reaching its climax in the final hymn of triumph –

'Thine be the glory, risen conquering Son'.

A great procession of people wound its way to Agherton cemetery, where all that was mortal of Bill Holley was laid to await the resurrection. It was a glorious June day. Swallows swooped over the open grave as one of his favourite choruses rang out with the glad assurance that had characterised his life and witness:

'He lives! He lives! Christ Jesus lives today!
He walks with me and talks with me
Along life's narrow way.
He lives! He lives! Salvation to impart.
You ask me how I know He lives?
He lives within my heart!'

Three days later, four thousand miles away, the church at Ochadamu was filled to overflowing for Igala's service of thanksgiving. Among many speakers, Elder Daniel Akwu recalled his recent visit to the Holley home. Then he told how he and Elder Achimugu had attended a service the following Sunday evening in Portstewart Baptist Church.

'Everyone was saying that Dr. Holley was a man of God,' he said. 'We were so happy to hear that in North-

ern Ireland, because that is how we will always remember him in Nigeria.'

Writing to Marion in September, as Secretary of the
Northern States Area Conference of the Qua Iboe
Church, Mr. Akwu paid further tribute to 'our dear Bill
Holley'.

'Among Igala Christians,' he wrote, 'Bill Holley's
name will ever be remembered for his selfless and con-
scientious service for God and humanity in Nigeria. He is
in his everlasting home now. That gives us unfathomable
joy. May God give the rest of us the same spiritual energy
so that we may be able to accomplish our tasks before
each one of us is called into eternal bliss with the Lord.'

In order to perpetuate Bill's memory it was decided
that, from January 1990, the Ochadamu Medical Centre
should be known as *Holley Memorial Hospital* – a fitting
and lasting tribute to the man who was

MORE THAN A DOCTOR

The Secret

WHAT, THEN, was the secret of Bill Holley's influence in so many different circles? What gave him such radiant joy, such compassion for the needy, such courage in the face of adversity? And what can we learn from his example?

Speaking to a group of young people in 1981, he described 'an important landmark in my spiritual experience'. It had occurred forty years earlier while stationed at the Simonstown naval base in South Africa. There he had heard a missionary speak about the secret of victorious Christian living, as taught by the apostle Paul in Romans chapter six and Galatians 2:20:

'Reckon yourselves to be dead indeed unto sin ....
yield yourselves unto God.'

'I am crucified with Christ: nevertheless I live; yet
not I, but Christ liveth in me: and the life which I now
live in the flesh I live by the faith of the Son of God,
who loved me and gave Himself for me.'

At the time of his conversion Bill had become intensely aware of the reality of Jesus as Saviour and Friend. Now he came to know Him as his very life. The old Bill Holley had been crucified with Christ on the cross. All that was necessary was to accept that fact by faith, and to yield himself, body, soul and spirit to the in-dwelling Christ, who was waiting to fill him with His own life and joy and power.

'What a wonderful message!' he recalled. 'Christian young people, read and re-read this truth till it gets into your mind, and ask God to transplant it into your heart.'

Then with typical honesty he added:

'I wish I could say that I have always lived in the light of that experience but, without a doubt, it has been a major influence in my life.'

'Christ liveth in me' – that was what made Bill Holley more than a doctor. That was why so many people in Nigeria and in Northern Ireland spoke of him as a man of God. That was why a fragrant wreath of flowers, laid on his grave by those who knew him best, bore the highest of all tributes:

'Thank you, Dad, for showing us Jesus'